TEACHING
COUNTING AND CARDINALITY
USING
LEGO® BRICKS

Dr. Shirley Disseler

COMPASS

Teaching Counting and Cardinality Using LEGO® Bricks

Copyright ©2017 by Shirley Disseler
Published by Brigantine Media/Compass Publishing
211 North Avenue, St. Johnsbury, Vermont 05819

Cover and book design by Anne LoCascio
Illustrations by Curt Spannraft
All rights reserved.

Brigantine Media/Compass Publishing
211 North Avenue
St. Johnsbury, Vermont 05819
Phone: 802-751-8802
Fax: 802-751-8804
E-mail: neil@brigantinemedia.com
Website: www.compasspublishing.org
www.brickmath.com

ORDERING INFORMATION
Quantity sales
Special discounts for schools are available for quantity purchases of physical books and digital downloads. For information, contact Brigantine Media at the address shown above or visit www.brickmath.com

Individual sales
Brigantine Media/Compass Publishing publications are available through most booksellers. They can also be ordered directly from the publisher.
Phone: 802-751-8802 | Fax: 802-751-8804
www.compasspublishing.org
www.brickmath.com
ISBN 978-1-9384066-3-8

CONTENTS

DEDICATION

In memory of my mother, who gave me passion for teaching children, and in honor of my dad, who continually inspires me to create!

INTRODUCTION

Counting seems like an easy task! But while many people think counting is the recitation of a numerical sequence, the concept is much more than mere number recognition. True understanding of ideas such as counting on, counting back, skip-counting, and one-to-one correspondence provide a solid base for numeracy. Learning to count on and to skip-count are precursors to adding. Learning to count back leads to understanding subtraction. While number recitation (rote counting) is an important skill, it does not provide actual understanding of counting and its role in further development of math skills.

Understanding the concepts of counting and cardinality builds a foundation of number sense, which is defined as: the ability to have flexibility and fluidity with numbers that leads to understanding how to use numbers to achieve sensible outcomes in mathematical situations (Burns, 2007; Carlyle and Mercado, 2012; Van de Walle, Karp, and Bay-Williams, 2012). Research has shown that having number sense and a full understanding of numeracy is key to a student's future mathematics achievement. Children who have a true fluid understanding of cardinality and counting concepts have an easier time with later mathematics concepts like multiplication and division.

The most recent research (Sylwester, 2000; Wolfe, 2010; Jensen, 2005) on the brain and learning mathematics stresses the need for interaction and stimulation with materials in the math environment in order for true learning to occur. *Teaching Counting and Cardinality Using LEGO® Bricks* provides activities that help children gain understanding

Burns, Marilyn. 2007. *About Teaching Mathematics: A K-8 Resource, 3rd Ed.* Sausalito, CA: Math Solutions.

Carlyle, Ann and Brenda Mercado. 2012. *Teaching Preschool and Kindergarten Math.* Sausalito, CA: Math Solutions.

Van de Walle, John A., Karen Karp, and Jennifer Bay-Williams. 2012. *Elementary and Middle School Mathematics: Teaching Developmentally, 8th Ed.* Pearson Education.

Sylwester, Robert. 2001. *A Biological Brain in a Cultural Classroom.* Thousand Oaks, CA: Corwin Press.

Wolfe, Patricia. 2010. *Brain Matters: Translating Research into Classroom Practice, 2nd Ed.* Alexandria, VA: Association for Supervision and Curriculum Development.

Jensen, Eric. 2005. *Teaching with the Brain in Mind.* 2nd Ed. Alexandria VA: Association for Supervision & Curriculum Development.

about the *why* and *how* of numbers. The activities are designed to offer the foundational understanding of number sense that leads to computational and mental math fluency in upper grades.

This book will help student master these topics, using a material found in almost every classroom and home— LEGO® bricks.

Why use LEGO® bricks to learn about counting and cardinality?

LEGO® bricks help students learn mathematical concepts through modeling. If a student can model a math problem, and then be able to understand and explain the model, he or she will begin the computational process without struggling.

Modeling with LEGO® bricks is an easy way for students to demonstrate their understanding of the vocabulary and the concepts of counting and cardinality.

LEGO® bricks are great tools for bringing many mathematical concepts to life: basic cardinality and counting, addition and subtraction, multiplication and division, fractions, data and measurement, and statistics and probability. Using LEGO® bricks fosters discussion, modeling, collaboration, and problem solving. These are the 21st century skills that will help students learn and be globally competitive.

The use of a common child's toy to do math provides a universal language for math. Children everywhere recognize this manipulative. It's fun to learn when you're using LEGO® bricks!

HOW TO TEACH WITH THE BRICK MATH SERIES

Using the *Teaching* and *Learning* Books:
Start by taking students through the **Part 1: Show Them How** section of each chapter. Build the models, show them to the students, and ask students questions. Where directed, have students build the same models themselves so they are manipulating the bricks as you are guiding them. A document camera is helpful to display your models to the whole class as you build them. The step-by-step directions in the *Teaching* books work through several problems in Part 1. If you are using the companion *Learning* books, which are the Student Editions, have students draw their models and answer the questions in those books as you teach using the *Teaching* book.

Once students have mastered the modeling processes from Part 1, move to the **Part 2: Show What You Know** section of the chapter. Ask students to complete each of the problems using bricks and drawing their models. The companion *Learning* books (Student Editions) have space for writing answers and baseplate paper for drawing models. Move through the room and check that students are building their models correctly, drawing them clearly, and understanding the concepts being taught.

The *Learning* books (Student Editions) include an assessment for each chapter, as well as additional problems for practice and challenge. The books also include an Assessment Chart to track each student's performance on all the skills taught in the *Counting and Cardinality* book.

Note: Active learning breeds active learners! Students will be motivated and engaged in math when they are using bricks. It will not be silent in your classroom, but it will be full of chatter about the math!

Suggested Bricks:

The Brick Math Series is designed to be used with basic LEGO® bricks. If you already have LEGO® bricks in your classroom, your students should be able to use them to make the models. They may have to combine smaller bricks together when the directions call for longer bricks such as 1x10s or 2x12s. Each student also needs a baseplate on which to build brick models.

Each chapter lists the bricks suggested for the lessons in that chapter for every two students, and the appendix includes a total brick inventory that lists all the bricks suggested for the program for every two students.

Specially designed Brick Math brick sets for one or two students are available for purchase from Brigantine Media. Brick sets are packaged in divided boxes and include a baseplate for each student.

Classroom Management Ideas:

- Before starting, have a conversation with the students about using bricks as a learning tool rather than a toy.
- Teach students the language of bricks (baseplate, stud, 1x1, 1x2, etc.).
- Assign brick sets to specific students and always give the same students the same sets. An easy way to do this is to number each brick set and assign the sets to pairs of students by number. When students know that they will always have to work with the same brick set, they are more likely to be careful that the bricks are returned to the set.
- Do not teach using bricks—or any manipulative—every day. Students also need to have opportunities to think through the math processes without having a physical object for modeling. Sometimes it helps to have students draw models without building them with bricks

first. Remember, they won't have access to manipulatives during most tests when they have to show what they have learned.

- To keep bricks clean: Put the bricks in a hosiery bag and wash them on the top rack of the dishwasher. Let them air dry. Clean bricks before assigning sets to new students.

- To keep bricks from sliding off desks, use foam shelf liner cut into rectangular pieces, or large meat trays (you can often get these free from a local supermarket).

- Inventory the sets twice a year and replace bricks as needed. There are a variety of vendors online that sell specific bricks, both new and used. LEGO® retail stores also sell a variety of individual bricks.

PATTERNS

Students will learn/discover:
- The meaning of the word *pattern*
- The link between different types of patterns

Why is this important?
Understanding patterns is a precursor to learning the mathematical concepts of addition, subtraction, and multiplication. Utilizing the teaching tools of color patterns, size patterns, and number patterns will lead to better understanding of skip-counting and jump numbers.

Vocabulary
- Pattern: a recurring form, design, or number representation

How to use the companion student book, *Learning Counting and Cardinality Using LEGO® Bricks*:
- After students build their models, have them draw the models and explain their thinking in the student book. Recording the models on paper after building them with bricks helps reinforce the concepts being taught.
- Discuss the vocabulary for each lesson with students as they work through the student book.
- Use the assessment in the student book to gauge student understanding of the content.

SUGGESTED BRICKS

Size	Number
1x1	20 of various colors (at least 5 of each color)
1x2	5
1x3	5
1x4	5
2x2	5
2x3	5
2x4	5

Note: Using a baseplate will help keep the bricks in a uniform line. One small baseplate is suggested for these activities.

Part 1: Show Them How

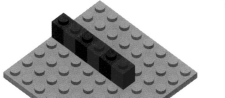

1. Build a **color pattern** model showing alternating colors and display it to the students.

Have students build and draw the model. Ask students to describe the model.

Discuss the word *pattern* with students. Have them identify your pattern. Using this illustration, students should identify it as blue, red, blue, red, blue, red, blue.

Ask students to describe what would be the next three colors in the pattern. Using this illustration, students should answer: blue, red, blue.

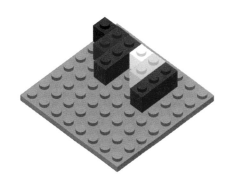

2. Build a **size pattern** model as shown in the illustration and display it to the students. *Note:* The colors of the bricks used for this pattern is not the critical element.

Have students build and draw the model. Ask students to describe the model.

Discuss the idea of different kinds of patterns. Explain that this pattern is based on brick size and the number of studs on each brick. Talk about this pattern using the brick vocabulary: this pattern shows 1 stud, 2 studs, and 3 studs with a 1x1 brick, a 1x2 brick, and a 1x3 brick, and is repeated once.

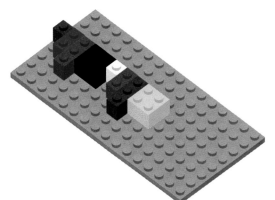

3. Build a **number pattern** model as shown in the illustration and display it to the students. *Note:* The colors of the bricks used for this pattern is not the critical element.

Ask students to describe the pattern.

Have students build and draw the model.

Discuss how the studs represent a number that can be counted. Practice counting using this model, having students point to each set of bricks that represent a term. Discuss that this pattern shows the terms 1, 2, 3, and 4, which are repeated once.

4. Build a **number and color pattern** model similar to the model shown in the illustration and display it to the students. *Note:* the colors and sizes of bricks used for this pattern are both important to the concept. Your model does not have to show these exact colors and sizes as illustrated, but should show a size progression and a specific color pattern.

Have students build the model, then draw their model. Ask students to describe the model. Students should understand that the pattern in this illustration shows the terms 1 white, 2 yellow, and 3 green, and is repeated once.

Note: This is a difficult task for students because it involves bringing two concepts together—number and color. This will likely require more discussion and additional modeling of similar patterns.

Part 2: Show What You Know

1. Can you build a pattern model that has four colors? Draw your model and describe the pattern.

Solutions will vary.

2. Can you build a pattern model that has at least three different sizes of bricks? Draw your model and describe the pattern.

Solutions will vary.

3. Can you build a number pattern model that shows 2, 4, 6, 2, 4, 6? Draw your model and describe the pattern.

4. Can you design and build a pattern model that is both a color pattern and a number pattern? Draw your model and describe the pattern.

Solutions will vary.

Challenge:

Design and build a pattern model. Find a partner. Exchange pattern models. Draw your partner's model and describe the pattern.

Solutions will vary.

SUGGESTED BRICKS

Size	Number
1x1	40
	(10 each of 4 different colors)

Note: Using a baseplate will help keep the bricks in a uniform line. Three small or one large baseplate is suggested for these activities.

WHAT IS A NUMBER?

Students will learn/discover:
- How to identify a number and link it to an object
- Basic counting of natural numbers 1 to 10

Why is this important?

Being able to assign a quantity or value to a numerical digit is a precursor to understanding numbers. This skill leads to understanding quantities that are "more than" or "less than" given amounts.

Vocabulary:
- Counting numbers: the list of natural numbers used to name objects one by one
- One-to-one correspondence: assigning or matching one item to one other item, or assigning one number to each object
- Studs: the round "bumps" on LEGO® bricks that are used as the counting unit

How to use the companion student book, *Learning Counting and Cardinality with LEGO® Bricks*:
- After students build their models, have them draw the models and explain their thinking in the student book. Recording the models on paper after building them with bricks helps reinforce the concepts being taught.
- Discuss the vocabulary for each lesson with students as they work through the student book.
- Use the assessment in the student book to gauge student understanding of the content.

Part 1: Show Them How

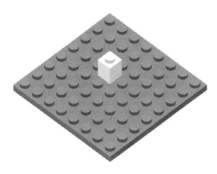

1. Place one 1x1 brick on a baseplate and display it to the students. *Note:* Use any color of 1x1 brick.

Ask students what they see. For this illustration, students should respond that they see one white brick.

Ask students how they know that the number represented is one. Answers may vary, but students should say that they can count only one stud, not simply one brick.

Discuss the brick vocabulary. Explain that the knobs on the top of the bricks are called *studs* and that the stud is the counting tool.

Have students place one finger on the top of the single stud and say "one stud." If you are using a document camera to display your model, ask one student to come up to the camera and show the class. If you are not using a document camera, have each student build the model with bricks.

Discuss the vocabulary term *one-to-one correspondence*. Explain that it means assigning one value or one description to each number of items.

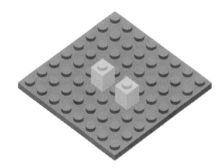

2. Place two 1x1 bricks on a baseplate and display the model to the students. *Note:* The two bricks should both be the same color. Use a different color from your model in step 1.

Have the students build the same model. Ask students to count and give a quantity for this model. For this illustration, students should respond, "two yellow studs" or "two yellow bricks."

Ask students what they notice that is different between the first model and this model. Students should notice there is one more brick and stud than the first model, and that the colors of bricks in the two models are different. They should talk about both the colors and the number of bricks and studs.

3. Place three 1x1 bricks on a baseplate and display the model to the students. *Note:* These three bricks should all be the same color. Use a different color from your models in steps 1 and 2.

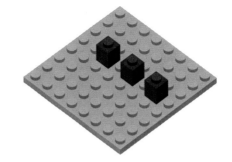

Have the students build the same model. Ask students how many studs they count on this model, and how this model is different from the previous model.

For this illustration, students should answer that there are three blue studs or bricks, with one more stud than on the previous model. Again, students should reference both color and number of studs and bricks in their answers.

4. Show the three models side by side.

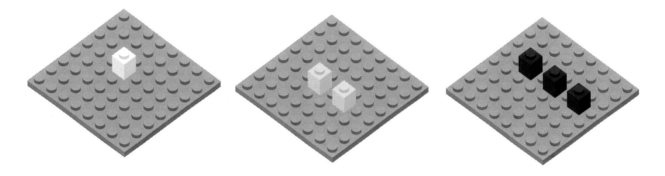

Ask students what they can say about these three models together.

Possible answers:
* Each model has one more than the one before it.
* The first model has 1 white stud, the second model has 2 yellow studs, and the third model has 3 blue studs.
* There is a space between each brick on the baseplates with two and three bricks.

Count the models in order based on the number of studs: 1 stud, 2 studs, 3 studs. *Note:* It is important to count using the frame of reference (studs), not the numerical digit alone.

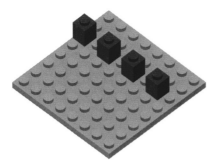

5. Ask students what they think the next model should look like.

Have students each build a model. Students should use four 1x1 bricks and put a space between each one. The students should use a fourth color of bricks, and the bricks in this model should all be the same color. Have each student draw his/her model.

Ask students: "How many studs are in this model?" Students should answer: "Four studs."

Ask students if this model has more studs or fewer studs than the other models. Students should answer: "More studs."

Have students say and write statements comparing the numbers of studs on each model.

Possible answers:
- The last model has one more than the model before it.
- The last model has two more than the second model.
- The last model has three more than the first model.
- All together there are 10 studs. (*Note:* This is an advanced answer and is not expected.)

Part 2: Show What You Know

1. Can you build a model that shows five studs? Use bricks that are all the same color. Build and draw your model. Describe your model and label each number.

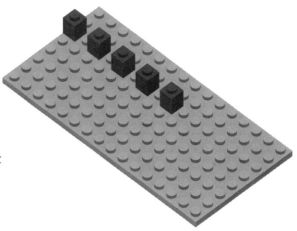

Answer: The model has five 1x1 bricks. They show that the number is 5 studs.

2. Can you build a model that shows one more stud than the model you just made? Build and draw your model and describe it.

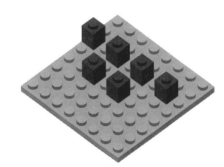

Answer: The model has 6 red bricks. Each brick has one stud. There are 6 studs altogether.

3. Can you build a model that has three more studs than the model you made in problem 1? Build and draw your model and describe it.

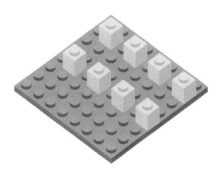

Answer: The model has eight 1x1 bricks. There are 8 studs in the model.

3

SUGGESTED BRICKS

Size	Number
1x1	40 (10 each of 4 different colors)
1x2	4 (same colors as 2x4 bricks)
1x3	8
2x2	4 (same colors as 2x3 bricks)
2x3	4 (same colors as 2x2 bricks)
2x4	4 (same colors as 1x2 bricks)

Note: Using a baseplate will help keep the bricks in a uniform line. One small baseplate is suggested for these activities.

TEN-FRAMES

Students will learn/discover:
- How to model numbers in sets of ten

Why is this important?
Being able to model numbers in the context of ten helps students formulate an understanding for number recognition. Use of the ten-frame model provides a base for seeing more than and less than ten, which is a prerequisite for building conceptual understanding of addition and subtraction.

Vocabulary:
- Ten-frame: a 2x5 model created with bricks
- More than
- Less than
- Ten

How to use the companion student book, *Learning Counting and Cardinality with LEGO® Bricks*:
- After students build their models, have them draw the models and explain their thinking in the student book. Recording the models on paper after building them with bricks helps reinforce the concepts being taught.
- Discuss the vocabulary for each lesson with students as they work through the student book.
- Use the assessment in the student book to gauge student understanding of the content.

Part 1: Show Them How

1. Build two *ten-frames* on a baseplate. Show your models to the students and have them each build two ten-frames. *Note:* A ten-frame has a 2x5-stud configuration, but there are no 2x5 LEGO® bricks. To build a ten-frame, use one 2x4 brick and one 1x2 brick of the same color or one 2x2 brick and one 2x3 brick of the same color.

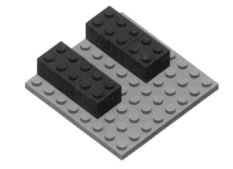

Ask students to count the number of studs in each ten-frame. Students should count 10. Discuss with them that this model is called a *ten-frame* and is used to model numbers in sets of ten.

2. Ask students to place one 1x1 brick on top of each stud in the first ten-frame.

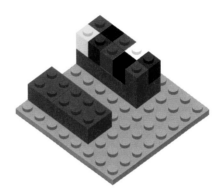

Students should be able to use one-to-one correspondence to count to ten. Have students draw their models.

3. Now work with the second ten-frame. Ask students to place enough 1x1 bricks to fill the top row of the second ten-frame. Have students write the number of studs used and draw their models. Students should count 5 studs.

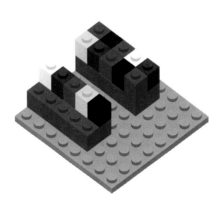

Ask students to look at both ten-frames. Have students count to determine which ten-frame models the larger number and explain why. Have students record their results in writing. Students should say that the top ten-frame models the larger number because it shows 10 studs, while the bottom one shows 5 studs.

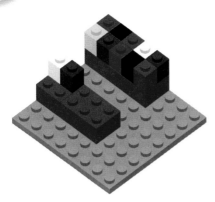

4. Clear the 1x1 bricks off your ten-frames and have the students clear their ten-frames.

Ask students to model the number 12 using two ten-frames. Have students draw their models.

Ask students how many studs are in their models. Students should answer that there are 12 studs. Discuss with students how they found 12. Did they count one by one, or did they fill in one full ten-frame, knowing that it represented the number 10, and then added 2 more? Discuss how this relates to the addition they will do later, such as 2 added to 10. Discuss how this relates to place value as 1 ten and 2 ones, which will be important as they start addition and subtraction.

5. Build another model using one or two ten-frames, but don't show it to the students. Have each student build his/her own model using one or two ten-frames. After students have completed their models, display your model and ask students whether their model is less than or more than your model.

Part 2: Show What You Know

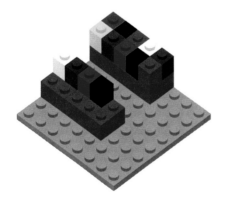

1. Can you build the number 14 using two ten-frame models? Draw your model. Label the model to show tens and ones.

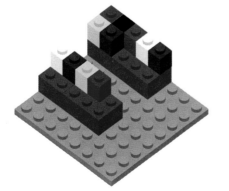

2. Using two ten-frames, can you build this model:

The first ten frame should show three more than the second ten frame. You must have at least two 1x1 bricks on the second ten-frame.

Draw your model and write the numbers that your model shows.

Answers will vary.

Sample solution

3. Ten-Frame Game:

    a. Each student builds a model of any number up to 20 using no more than two ten-frames.

    b. Find a partner who has a model that shows a number more than yours.

    c. Find a partner who has a model that shows a number equal to yours.

    d. Find a partner who has a model that shows a number less than yours.

Challenges:

Tens:
10 studs

Tens:
10 studs

Ones:
4 studs

4. Build four ten-frames. Can you model the number 24? Draw your model and label the tens and ones.

Answer: Students should identify that each ten-frame represents a set of 10. There are 2 of those sets, which makes 20. The third ten-frame has 4 single studs to represent the 4 in 24.

Note: Students approaching proficiency in counting should be able to count 10, 20, 21, 22, 23, 24.

5. Choose a number greater than 24. Can you model your number? Build and draw your model. Explain your model.

Answers will vary.

4

SUGGESTED BRICKS

Size	Number
1x1	10
1x2	10
1x3	8
1x4	8
1x6	8
1x8	4
1x10	4
1x12	4
2x2	4
2x4	8
2x8	2

Note: Using a baseplate will help keep the bricks in a uniform line. One small baseplate is suggested for these activities.

SKIP-COUNTING

Students will learn/discover:
How to skip-count by 2s, 3s, 5s, and 10s

Why is this important?
Skip-counting is a prerequisite to mastering multiplication based upon repeated addition models. At an early age, students should be able to skip-count by 2s, 3s, 5s, and 10s. Students in early grades (K-2) are preparing for the idea of multiplication from a set perspective. Skip-counting leads to set models. Also, repeated addition models based on skip-counting on a number line provide a visual representation of what is happening when jumps are made in equivalent increments.

Vocabulary:
- Skip-counting: Counting by a number other than 1 (i.e., by 2s, by 3s, etc.)
- More than
- Greater than

How to use the companion student book, *Learning Counting and Cardinality with LEGO® Bricks*:
- After students build their models, have them draw the models and explain their thinking in the student book. Recording the models on paper after building them with bricks helps reinforce the concepts being taught.
- Discuss the vocabulary for each lesson with students as they work through the student book.
- Use the assessment in the student book to gauge student understanding of the content.

Part 1: Show Them How

1. Build a model of skip-counting by 2s and show it to the students. Have each student build the same model.

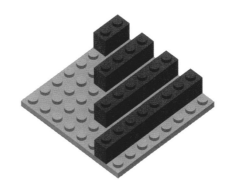

Ask students what they notice about this model. Possible responses include:
- It looks like a stair step from smallest to largest.
- Each one is two more than the one before it.
- There are eight studs in the longest column.

2. Explain to students that this is a model of skip-counting by 2s. Have them count with you aloud: "two studs, four studs, six studs, eight studs."

3. Ask students what number would come next in the model. *Note:* This provides background for identifying patterns in mathematics.

Students should determine that the next number would be 10.

Add a column of ten studs to your model while students do the same to their models. *Note:* Use a combination of bricks to build the 1x10 configuration, if necessary. It may be clearer to students if all bricks used are the same color.

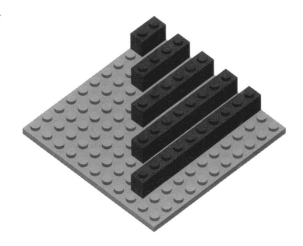

Skip-count aloud with students: "two studs, four studs, six studs, eight studs, ten studs."

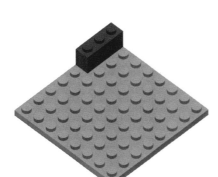

4. Start to build a model of skip-counting by 3s. Show the first 1x3 brick. Have students build the same model.

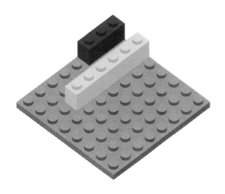

5. Ask students what brick is added next to a model showing skip-counting by 3s.

Have students find one brick (or a combination of bricks) and add it to their models. Do the same to your model and display it.

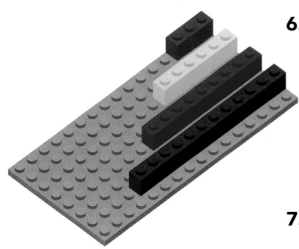

6. Ask students to model the next two steps in skip-counting by 3s.

Check student models to make sure they have successfully added bricks showing 9 studs and 12 studs to their models. *Note:* Students will have to use combinations of bricks to make a 1x9 column of bricks and possibly 1x12. It may be clearer to students if all bricks used in each column are the same color.

7. Have students count aloud by 3s and touch each column of bricks as they count: "three studs, six studs, nine studs, twelve studs."

8. Ask students how many studs are needed to model the next number in the skip-counting by 3s. Students should answer: 15 studs.

Have students add a column of bricks equaling 15 studs to their models. Do the same to your model and display it. *Note:* Students will have to use combinations of bricks to make a 1x15 column of bricks. It may be clearer to students if all bricks used are the same color.

Part 2: Show What You Know

1. Can you build a model that shows skip-counting by 4s? Build at least three steps. Draw your model and label it to show how you counted.

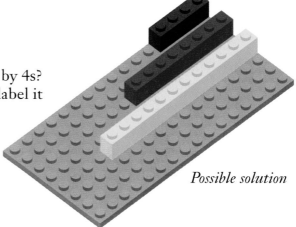

Possible solution

2. Can you build a model that shows skip-counting by 5s? Build at least three steps. Draw your model and label it to show how you counted.

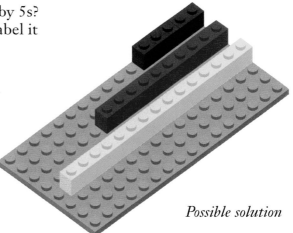

Possible solution

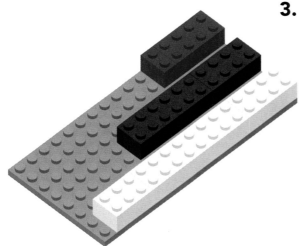

Possible solution

3. Can you build a model that shows skip-counting by 10s? Build at least three steps. Draw your model and label it to show how you counted.

4. Choose a number. Do not tell anyone your number. Can you model a skip-counting pattern with your secret number? Show your partner your model and have your partner identify the skip-count pattern.

Answers will vary.

JUMP NUMBERS

SUGGESTED BRICKS

Size	Number
1x1	10
1x2	6
1x3	2
2x2	4
2x3	6
2x4	8
2x6	2
2x8	2
2x10	2

Note: Using a baseplate will help keep the bricks in a uniform line. One large baseplate is suggested for these activities.

5

Students will learn/discover:
- How to count forward and backward from a given number (sometimes called "counting on" and "counting back")
- Skip-counting and jump numbers
- Patterns of even and odd numbers

Why is this important?
A true understanding of cardinality depends on one's ability to understand absolute location of a number on a number line. Students need to understand how to count forward and backward from any given number. One way to learn this is by counting the number of "jumps" by a specific number (called "skip-counting" if the jumps are all the same).

Vocabulary:
- Odd: numbers that are not divisible evenly by two and always have leftover studs when modeled with bricks
- Even: numbers divisible by two or ending in zero
- Skip-counting: counting by the same number (greater than 1) each time
- Jump numbers: the number of skip-counts needed to reach a solution, which can include adding leftovers as jumps at the end
- More than: comparison of amounts that includes a greater number of items than the original amount
- Less than: comparison of amounts that includes fewer items than the original amount

How to use the companion student book, *Learning Counting and Cardinality with LEGO® Bricks*:

- After students build their models, have them draw the models and explain their thinking in the student book. Recording the models on paper after building them with bricks helps reinforce the concepts being taught.
- Discuss the vocabulary for each lesson with students as they work through the student book.
- Use the assessment in the student book to gauge student understanding of the content.

Part 1: Show Them How

1. Build a brick number line model and show it to the students.

Note: Use the same color of bricks to represent a given number. Vary the colors from number to number. Any colors of bricks may be used.

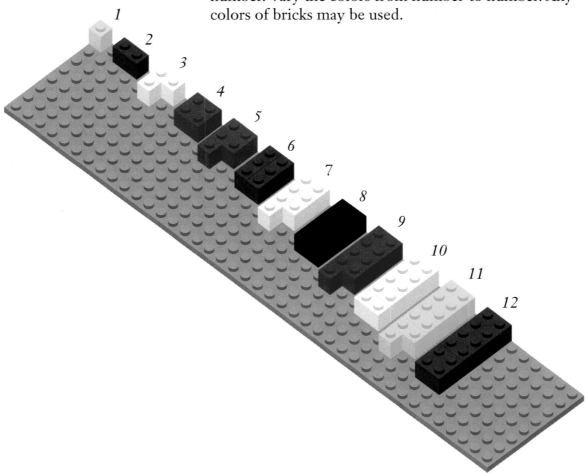

Point to each brick and count based on the number of studs shown. Have students count aloud from 1 to 12, using studs as the reference point ("one stud, two studs, three studs," etc.).

Ask students how to count to the end if you begin with the brick that represents 8. Students should count "eight, nine, ten, eleven, twelve." Discuss that counting forward from a given number on the number line helps with addition. Note that there are 4 spaces between 8 and 12, showing that 8 + 4 = 12.

2. Build a model of counting by 2s and show it to the students. Have students build the model, then draw and label it. *Note:* Use the same color of bricks to represent a given number. Vary the colors from number to number. Any colors of bricks may be used.

Discuss how jump numbers relate to skip-counting. Students should understand that skip-counting is always done in equivalent increments, whereas jumps might not always be equivalent.

Students should be able to count the number of jumps and describe the pattern as skip-counting or by its pattern. For example, in the model of counting by 2s, there are four jumps in the skip-counting pattern of 2s. For a pattern of 2, 5, 7, 10, there are three jumps and the pattern is *jump 1 = 3, jump 2 = 2, jump 3 = 3*.

Ask students what number comes next in the model of counting by 2s, and have them explain how they know the answer. *Note:* Have students touch the bricks as they count the jumps.

Students should say that the next number in the pattern is 12. They know it is 12 because there are 2 between each number, and 2 more than 10 is 12.

3. Build a model to show counting by 4s. Have students build a model to show counting by 4s, then draw and label it.

Ask students how many jumps there are in the pattern. Students should answer 3, and touch the bricks as they count the jumps.

Ask students what number comes next in the pattern, and how they know the answer. Have students model the pattern, then draw their model and label it.

Students should know that the next number is 20, because there are 4 between each number, and 4 more than 16 is 20. Students should model 20 with bricks in a 2x10 configuration.

4. Have students work in pairs to build one even number model (2, 4, 6, 8, 10, and 12) and one odd number model (1, 3, 5, 7, 9, and 11). *Note:* Students should not use 1x3, 1x4, 1x6, 1x8, or 1x10 bricks to build these models.

Even numbers

Odd numbers

Ask students how the model for 2, 4, 6, 8, 10, and 12 is different from the model for 1, 3, 5, 7, 9, and 11. Students should recognize that all the even numbers are modeled by rectangles, and the odd number models each have an "extra" brick. Discuss the even and odd number models to be sure all students understand the differences between them.

Part 2: Show What You Know

1. Build a brick number line that shows 1 to 10. Begin at the brick that represents the number 3. Counting by 2s, can you find the next three numbers in the sequence? Draw and label your model.

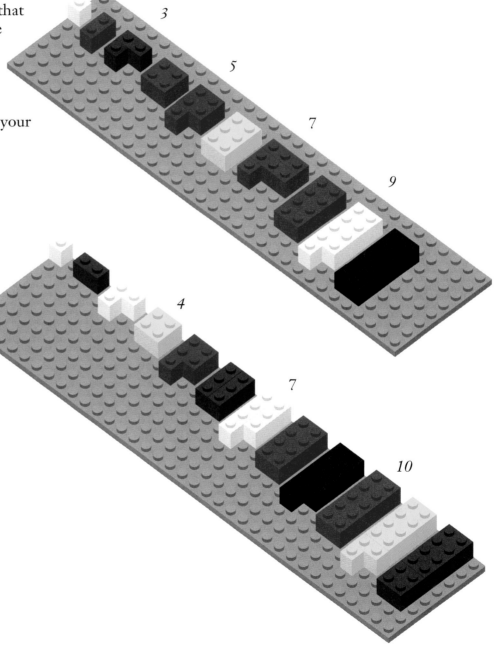

2. Build a brick number line that shows 1 to 12. Begin at the brick that represents the number 4. Counting by 3s, can you find the next two numbers in the sequence?

3. Using the number line for 1 to 12, begin at the number 2. Can you find jumps of 2 until the end of the number line? How many jumps of 2 are there in the sequence? Draw your model and label each jump of 2.

Answer: There are 5 jumps of 2 from the numbers 2 to 12.

2

4

6

8

10

12

4. Can you build one model that shows both even and odd numbers? Draw and label the model with numbers, showing which are even and odd.

Answers will vary, but check that students can make their own decisions about odd and even numbers and model them correctly.

SQUARE NUMBERS

6

Size	Number
1x1	20
1x2	10
1x3	8
1x4	8
2x2	8
2x3	4
2x4	2

Note: Using a baseplate will help keep the bricks in a uniform line. One large baseplate is suggested for these activities.

Students will learn/discover:
- How to use a variety of bricks to model numbers up to 20
- What a square number looks like in a model

Why is this important?

This lesson will help students develop number sense as they begin to understand vocabulary required for later mathematical number skills. Students at this stage are not yet learning what it means to say a number is squared. Rather, recognizing a model of a square number versus a non-square number creates discussion around patterns, models of numbers, and lays the groundwork for advanced numerical vocabulary. These skills help students find meaning in addition and multiplication.

Vocabulary:
- Modeling
- More than
- Less than
- Same
- Square number pattern
- Compare

How to use the companion student book, *Learning Counting and Cardinality with LEGO® Bricks*:
- After students build their models, have them draw the models and explain their thinking in the student book. Recording the models on paper after building them with bricks helps reinforce the concepts being taught.
- Discuss the vocabulary for each lesson with students as they work through the student book
- Use the assessment in the student book to gauge student understanding of the content.

Part 1: Show Them How

1. Using bricks, build models of various numbers up to 10. Show models to the students. The models demonstrate various ways students might think about the numbers.

Examples of models include:

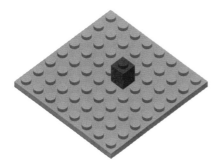 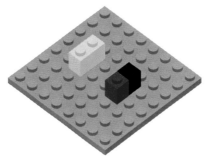 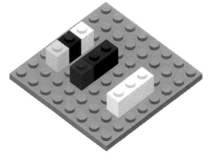

The number 1 built with one 1x1 brick

The number 2 built two different ways: one 1x2 brick and two 1x1 bricks

The number 3 built three different ways: three 1x1 bricks, one 1x2 and one 1x1 brick, and one 1x3 brick.

2. Review with students how to count studs using one-to-one correspondence. Tell students that they will be using this idea to model larger numbers and compare size. *Note:* This will lead to a later understanding of square numbers and multiplication.

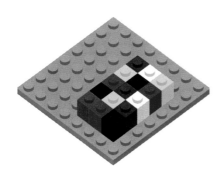

3. Build a model of the number 15 using 1x1 bricks (3 across and 5 down) and show it to the students. Ask students to build the model.

4. Ask students to describe the shape they see in the model. Students should answer: A rectangle with the top and bottom shorter in length than the left and right sides.

Ask students which bricks were used to make 15 in this model. Students should answer: Fifteen 1x1 bricks.

5. Ask students to rearrange the 1x1 bricks on their baseplate to build another model of 15 that looks different than the last model of 15. Ask students to draw their model and describe it.

Ask students how this model is like the previous one and how it is different from that model. Students' models can vary widely from the previous model. If they build a rectangle with a horizontal orientation, they will describe it as opposite from the vertical one. If students build an irregular shape with the 15 bricks, they will describe it by side lengths.

6. Ask students to build a model of the number 13 using 1x1 bricks. Ask students to describe how this model is different from the model of 15 that they built. Have students draw their models.

Students should discuss leftover bricks. They should see that you can not make a rectangle with this number because it is prime. *Note:* Students are not able to express the idea of prime and composite yet, but this activity will lead to that theoretical understanding later.

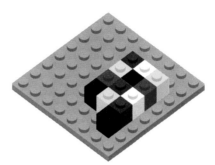

Possible model

7. Have students build a model of 2 using one 1x2 brick. Walk around and check student models to see how they are approaching this task and to make sure they are using the correct brick. Build a model or have a student show one that he/she has built.

Ask students to describe the shape they see. Students should say that the shape is a rectangle.

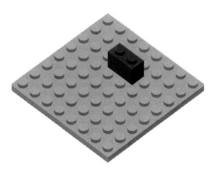

8. Ask students to build another model by taking two more 1x2 bricks and placing them together on the baseplate. Ask students what number this represents. Students should answer: the number 4.

Ask students to compare this model to the 1x2 brick that models the number 2. Students should answer that this model has two more studs, or note that it looks like a square. Have students draw the model and write a description.

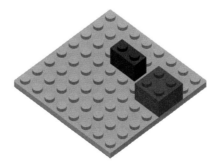

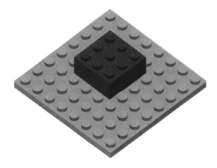

9. Tell students they are going to build another model that forms a square. Ask students to build a model of 9 using three 1x3 bricks. Walk around and investigate how students are approaching this task. Ask students questions individually to guide them, such as:

- How are you thinking about the number 9?
- Is 9 an odd number or an even number?
- Are there any ways to model 9 other than what you have created?

Ask students how this model is like the model for 4 that they built. Students should answer that this model is also in the shape of a square.

Have students draw their models and write a description.

Part 2: Show What You Know

1. Using 1x4 bricks, can you build a model showing 12 studs? Draw your model.

How many bricks did you use? Write a description of your model. Is your model a square or a rectangle?

Answer: It takes three 1x4 bricks to model 12 in the shape of a rectangle.

2. Using 1x1 bricks, can you build a model of the number 17? Draw your model. Compare your model with a partner. Discuss how the models are alike and different. What do you notice about both your model and your partner's model? Write a description of your model.

Answer: Models will vary, but students should recognize that no model of 17 can be a square and that there are leftover bricks.

3. Can you build a model of another square number? Choose a number other than 4 or 9. Draw your model. Explain why it is a square number.

Answers will vary.

4. Choose a number greater than 10. Build a model of your number using bricks. Then:
- Find someone who has the *same* number model as you.
- Find someone who built a model that shows a number *greater than* yours.
- Find someone who built a model that shows a number *less than* yours.

SUGGESTED BRICKS

Size	Number
1x1	20 (5 each of 4 different colors)
1x2	5
1x3	10
1x4	5
2x2	5
2x4	5
2x6	2

Note: Using a baseplate will help keep the bricks in a uniform line. One small baseplate is suggested for these activities.

MORE THAN/ LESS THAN

Students will learn/discover:
- The meaning of the words *more than* and *less than*
- The link between *more than* and *greater than*
- The link between *less than* and *fewer than*

Why is this important?
The ideas of *more than* and *less than* help students progress toward the concepts of addition and subtraction. Understanding sets that have *more than* or *less than* are important for comparing numbers throughout the mathematics curriculum.

Vocabulary
- More than
- Less than
- Compare

How to use the companion student book, *Learning Counting and Cardinality with LEGO® Bricks*:
- After students build their models, have them draw the models and explain their thinking in the student book. Recording the models on paper after building them with bricks helps reinforce the concepts being taught.
- Discuss the vocabulary for each lesson with students as they work through the student book.
- Use the assessment in the student book to gauge student understanding of the content.

Part 1: Show Them How

1. Build a model of a 9-stud square and label it *A*. Display your model to the class using a document camera or have students build the model themselves. Ask students to identify the number of studs in model A.

Have students write the number of studs. Show students how to record evidence. Students should write, "Model A has 9 studs."

As a review, ask students to describe the shape of the model. Students should recognize that the model is in the shape of a square.

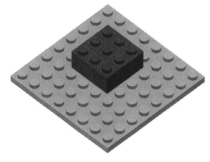

Model A

2. Build another model that shows 10 by adding one 1x1 brick to the 9-stud square model, and label it *B*. Show it to the students or have them build their own models.

Ask students to describe this model. Students might answer that it has one more stud than the previous model or that is has one stud left over.

Have students draw the model and describe it in writing. Students should write, "Model B has 10 studs."

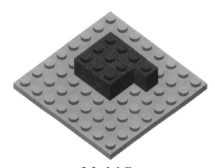

Model B

3. Discuss the concept of *more than* with the class. Build a model that has 12 studs and label it *C*. Show it to the students or have them build their own models.

Ask students to describe how many more studs this model shows than the first model. Students should answer that Model C has 3 more studs than Model A.

Discuss that the word *studs* gives the number 3 a frame of reference.

If students are ready for math symbols, show them the *greater than* symbol (>). Have students write a math sentence in their journal using the symbol.
(*Answer*: C > A or 12 studs > 9 studs)

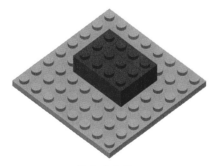

Model C

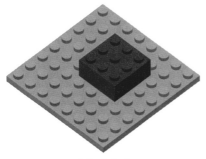

Model A

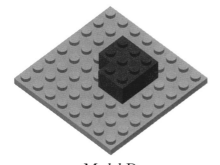

Model D

4. Show students model A again. Build a model that shows one less than the original model and label it *D*. Ask students what they can say about this model.

Students could answer that it has one less than the first model, or note that it is not a square number because it has leftovers.

Ask students to describe how they know Model D has less than Model A. Have students justify and provide evidence of understanding by drawing the model and writing about it.

If students are ready, show them the *less than* symbol (<). Have students write a math statement using the symbols for these models. (*Answer:* D < A or 8 studs < 9 studs)

5. Introduce the word *compare*. Tell students that by looking at the number of studs on the models we can compare the amounts they represent or show. Using the math symbols is the way to show comparisons between numbers. Tell students that when we use the symbols in math for comparing, we call them *greater than* (>) and *less than* (<).

6. Build a model of 14 studs and a model of 12 studs as illustrated. Label the model of 14 studs *E*. Label the model of 12 studs *F*. Show the models to the students or have them build their own models. Have them write one *more than* statement and one *less than* statement about the models.

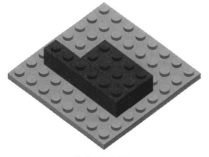

Model E

Possible answers include:
- Model E is greater than (more than) model F; 14 is greater than 12; E > F; or 14 > 12.
- Model F is less than model E; 12 is less than 14; F < E; or 12 < 14.

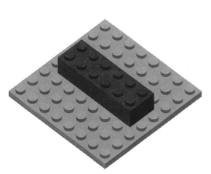

Model F

Part 2: Show What You Know

1. Build models of two numbers. Label your models A and B. Draw your models.

Can you write a *more than* statement about your models?

Answers will vary.

2. Build models of two numbers you did not use in problem 1. Label your models C and D. Draw your models.

Can you write a *less than* statement about your models?

Answers will vary.

3. Build a comparison model using two different numbers. Draw your model.

Can you write two math statements using symbols for these models that show *less than* and *greater than*?

Answers will vary.

Challenge:

Make a model of three different numbers. Draw your models.

Write as many math sentences as you can about these number models.

Answers will vary. Note: Most students will compare their first and second models, their second and third models, and their third and first models in three separate statements. Students will only write a sentence that uses two symbols if they are ready.

APPENDIX

- **Suggested Brick Inventory**
- **Student Assessment Chart**
- **Baseplate Paper**

SUGGESTED BRICK INVENTORY

SIZE	NUMBER
1x1	84 (32 each of two colors and 10 each of two more colors)
1x2	25 (10 each of two colors and 5 of a third color)
1x3	12 (6 each of two colors)
1x4	10
1x6	10
1x8	6
1x10	6
1x12	5
1x16	2
2x2	12
2x3	6
2x4	9
2x6	4
2x8	2
2x10	2

COUNTING AND CARDINALITY
Student Assessment Chart

Name _____

Performance Skill	Not yet	With help	On target	Comments
I can count from 1 to 10.				
I can count objects by number.				
I can make a pattern using brick colors.				
I can make a pattern using studs to show numbers.				
I can skip-count by 2, 3, 5, and 10.				
I can count jumps between numbers on a number line.				
I can make a set of tens on a ten frame and count tens and ones.				
I can tell the name of a number in the tens place and in the ones place.				
I can identify numbers that are even and odd.				

BASEPLATE PAPER

BASEPLATE PAPER

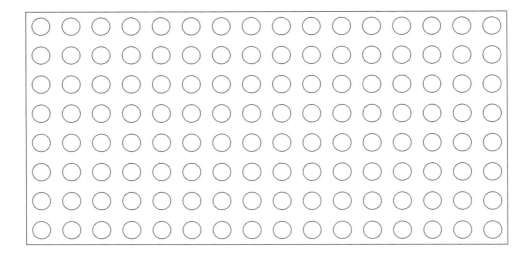

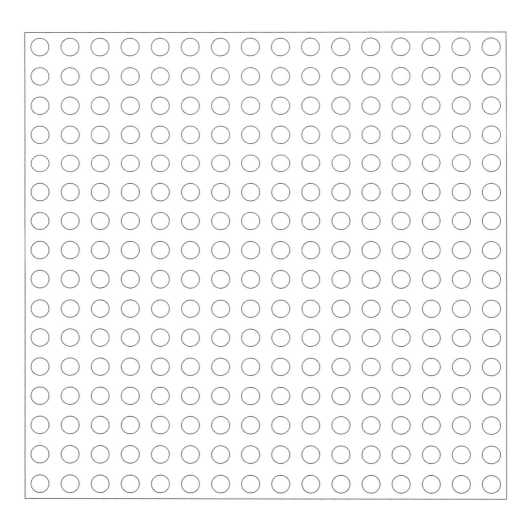